j568
WIT

Witmer, Lawrence M.

The search for the
origin of birds.

$25.90   08/26/1998

DATE			

The Search for the Origin of Birds

THE SEARCH FOR THE ORIGIN OF BIRDS

By Lawrence M. Witmer, Ph.D.
Illustrated by Kit Mather

PREHISTORIC LIFE
FRANKLIN WATTS
NEW YORK/LONDON/HONG KONG/SYDNEY
DANBURY, CONNECTICUT

For Sam

Photograph p. 24, copyright © Sinclair Stammers/Photo Researchers/SPL

Library of Congress Cataloging-in-Publication Data

Witmer, Lawrence M.
The search for the origin of birds / Lawrence M. Witmer: illustrated by Kit Mather.
p. cm. — (Prehistoric life)
Includes bibliographical references and index.
Summary: Discusses the facts and clues used to formulate the various theories of the origin of birds.
ISBN 0-531-11232-2
1. Birds, Fossil — Juvenile literature. 2. Birds — Origin — Juvenile literature. [1. Birds — Origin. 2. Birds, Fossil. 3. Prehistoric animals.] I. Mather, Kit, ill. II. Title. III. Series.
QE871.W58 1995   95-14635
568—dc20   CIP   AC

Contents

1

The Problem of Origins

9

2

Archosauria: The Extended Family of the Birds

17

3

Archaeopteryx, Compsognathus,
and the Dinosaurian Origin of Birds

22

4

***Euparkeria* and the**
Pseudosuchian Origin of Birds

30

5

The Crocodylomorph Origin of Birds

33

6
Deinonychus and the
New Dinosaurian Origin
of Birds
36

7
Agreement?
40

8
The Origin of Flight
in Birds
47

9
Conclusion:
But How Do We Know?
53

Glossary
58

For Further
Reading
60

Index
61

The Search for the Origin of Birds

1
The Problem of Origins

Birds seem somehow strange. If you think about it for a minute, they seem almost bizarre in comparison to us and to the animals that live alongside us — such as dogs and cats. Birds are warm-blooded, as we are, but have feathers and scales instead of fur or hair. They have horny bills instead of teeth. They do complicated things, such as building intricate nests and singing elaborate songs, but their intelligence seems much different from our own. Obviously, the thing that really sets birds apart is that they fly — and this unusual manner of getting around affects virtually every aspect of their drastically different **anatomy**.

We're mammals, so we tend to think of ourselves — and of other large, impressive mammals such as lions, bears, buffaloes, and elephants — as being the dominant creatures living on land. However, in many ways, birds, not mammals, can claim this title. Birds are at or near the top of the food chain in most animal communities. Perhaps more importantly, there are more than twice as many kinds of birds as there are mammals, and there are more than 300 billion individual birds living today!

Birds truly stand apart from other animals. To understand birds — to see how they came to be so different, so diverse, so dominant — we need to understand their **origin**. So, how do we investigate this? How do we bridge the gap between birds and other animals to find their closest relatives and, ultimately, their **ancestors**? In fact, how do we discover the "family" relationships and origin of *any* group of **organisms**?

This problem of "origins" is quite tricky. The origin of any group of animals or plants is in the past, so nobody living today was there actually to see it happen. To investigate origins, scientists need to use a sort of detective work to first find clues, and then interpret them. The next step — and the most important one — is to construct a "family tree" from these clues. Family trees show who is related to whom. We can then trace back along the "branches" of the tree to the "trunk." At the base of the trunk will be the ancestor.

We do something similar when we trace our own origins — to find our ancestors beyond our parents, grandparents, or great-grandparents. To draw a human family tree, we look for clues in written records in hospitals, courthouses, churches, and other places. Unfortunately, there are no clear birth certificates or other records to help us draw a bird family tree.

What kind of clues, then, are available to our scientific detective? First, we look at the anatomical characteristics of living organisms — how the parts of the body are shaped and fit together. Second, we look at

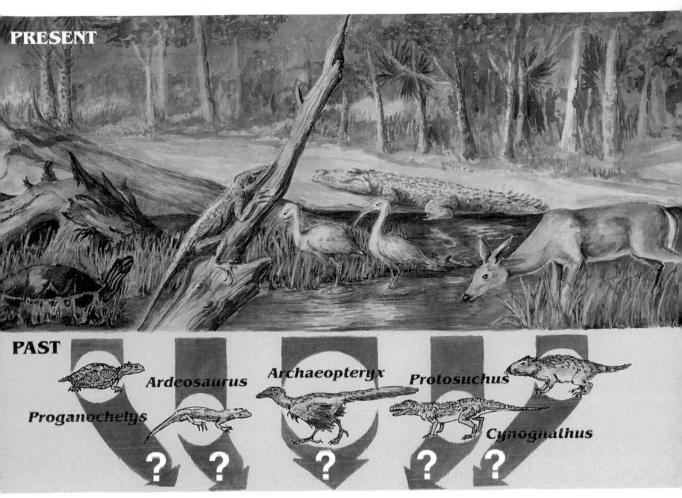

PRESENT

PAST

Proganochelys

Ardeosaurus

Archaeopteryx

Protosuchus

Cynognathus

? ? ? ? ?

THE PROBLEM OF ORIGINS

All the diverse animals living today have a common
evolutionary origin. We must put together clues from
living and fossil animals in our search for origins.

the **fossil** evidence of **extinct** organisms. Although
humans were not around for the origin of most groups,
other types of organisms did exist. Their fossils may
provide important clues. We'll probably never be lucky
enough to find the fossils of the true ancestor of birds.
Our hope is that we *will* discover which of the extinct

groups is closest to that ancestor. The "clues" we look for are usually in the form of similarities. In other words, we use characteristics that are *similar* among groups of organisms as a key to discovering relationships.

The guiding principle in interpreting these clues is **evolution**. Organisms that evolved from the same ancestor (called the "common ancestor") usually share various similar characteristics. This is why we (and our brothers and sisters) look more like our parents — our common ancestors — than some unrelated stranger does. Similarities that result from common ancestry are called **homologies**.

However, not all similar characteristics are the result of common ancestry. Sometimes similar features appear through independent evolution in separate groups. These similarities are called **convergences**. Convergence usually comes about when different kinds of animals become adapted to the same environment or lifestyle. For example, dolphins evolved from land-living mammals but developed fins that are convergent with those of fish, because both dolphins and fish swim better with fins.

As another example, let's compare the similar looking wing skeletons of an ostrich, a crow, and a bat. Although ostriches don't fly, they share with crows (and all other living birds) a unique similarity of the major hand bone. This similarity results from common ancestry, and so is a homologous similarity. Therefore, the wings of ostriches and crows are homologous. The peculiar hand bone evolved as an adaptation for flight, so this tells us that ostriches lost the power of flight at some point in their evolution. In contrast, although both bats and crows use their wings for flight, the con-

Convergence: Dolphins (top) are mammals, and sharks (bottom) are fish, but both evolved similar, streamlined body plans.

struction of their wing skeletons is different. This tells us that wings in bats and in birds evolved as the result of convergence.

Common ancestry is the key. Crow and ostrich wings are homologous because their common ancestor had wings. The unusual hand bone provides the important clue. However, the common ancestor of bats and birds lacked wings, so bird and bat wings must be convergences.

13

In looking at origins, we need to distinguish between homologous similarities and convergent similarities. However, not all homologous similarities are the same. The most helpful homologous similarities are the ones that came about in the evolution of a "new" feature — that is, an evolutionary **specialization** or **derived character**. Shared **primitive characters** give us less useful information. Let's use the previous example to understand these ideas.

Ostriches, crows, and bats all have two bones in the forearm. In fact, all land-living animals with a backbone have two bones in the forearm. So, it's a homologous similarity of ostriches, crows, and bats. However, it's also a *primitive* character, and so it doesn't tell us anything about the relationship of ostriches, crows, and bats, because all three have the same two forearm bones. The unusual hand bone, however, is a *derived* character that only birds have. It shows that ostriches and crows are more closely related to each other than either is to bats.

The situation is often messy when you look at many characters and groups of organisms. We usually look at all the clues together when constructing family trees. Because it's sometimes hard to know whether the similarities are from common ancestry or convergence, or are derived or primitive, we sometimes draw more than one family tree. Then, we choose the family tree that is supported by the largest number of similarities that are both derived and homologous. For example, the theory that ostriches and crows are closely related might seem unlikely since crows and bats fly and ostriches don't. In other words, we might be tempted to think that crows and bats are closely related because they fly, and that ostriches are more distant relatives

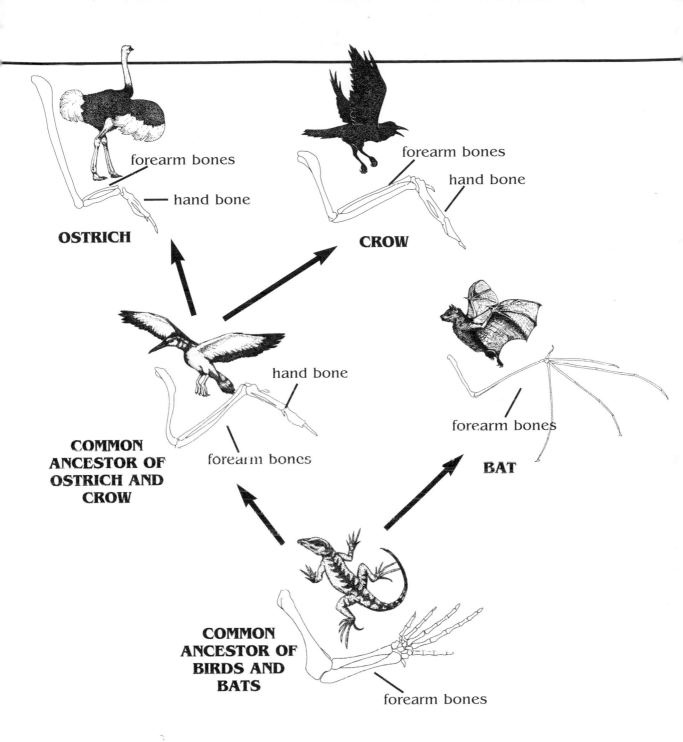

OSTRICH

forearm bones

hand bone

CROW

forearm bones

hand bone

COMMON ANCESTOR OF OSTRICH AND CROW

hand bone

forearm bones

BAT

forearm bones

COMMON ANCESTOR OF BIRDS AND BATS

forearm bones

Homology versus convergence: Ostrich and crow wings are **homologous** because their ancestor (middle left) *had* wings, but bat and bird wings are **convergent** because their ancestor (bottom) *lacked* wings.

Primitive versus derived: Having two forearm bones is a **primitive** feature that tells us nothing about how ostriches, crows, and bats are related, but the unique hand bone is a **derived** feature found only in birds because they don't fly. The theory, however, is supported by more clues (derived homologies) than just the peculiar hand bone. In fact, there are so many such clues (feathers, no teeth, and more) that the theory must be correct.

Looking at living forms (like ostriches, crows, and bats) really only gives us a partial view of the whole range of life's diversity. Many types of organisms are extinct and have vanished from the Earth. In fact, some scientists have estimated that 99 percent of all types of organisms that have ever existed are now extinct! The fossil remains of these extinct groups can help to fill in gaps in our knowledge.

For the scientific detective searching for origins, fossils are important because fossils tend to have a greater number of primitive features than do living organisms. Unfortunately, there's no guarantee that fossils will be primitive in all (or even many) features. Also, because fossilization is a rare event, we might never be lucky enough to find the fossil of an actual ancestor — but we might get close. We'll see that our search for the origin of birds has taken several turns over the years, usually because of the discovery of new, important fossils.

To sum up, finding the origin of anything is hard, and the origin of birds is no exception. The procedure is to look at the characteristics of living and fossil groups of organisms. We then decide which characteristics are primitive or derived, and homologous or convergent. We use the derived homologies to draw a family tree, and this family tree allows us to create a picture of what the ancestor might have looked like. We'll have then found the origin we searched for. It sounds easy, but as we use this procedure to explore the origin of birds we'll find the path a little rough going at times.

2
Archosauria: The Extended Family of Birds

Where do birds fit into the big picture of life on Earth? Birds lack the derived specializations we see in many of the major groups of animals. For example, they don't have fur as mammals do, or bony shells like turtles. So they are neither mammals nor turtles. They share a number of primitive characteristics with reptiles like lizards and crocodiles, such as egg-laying, scaly feet, and some other features, but again, these primitive characteristics don't tell us much. Birds do, however, have some features — such as a peculiar opening in the bony snout — that are derived evolutionary specializations found only in a group of animals called **archosaurs**. Archosauria is an unfamiliar name for a familiar group of animals. Since several groups of archosaurs have been suggested to be closely related to birds, we'll look briefly at the major groups of archosaurs.

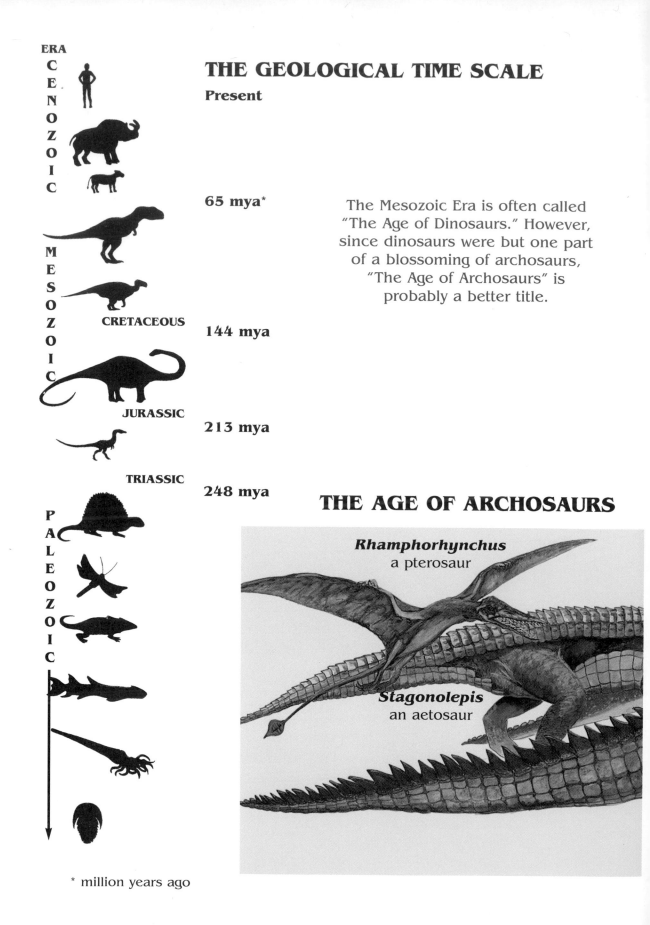

THE GEOLOGICAL TIME SCALE

ERA

Present

C E N O Z O I C

65 mya*

M E S O Z O I C

CRETACEOUS

144 mya

JURASSIC

213 mya

TRIASSIC

248 mya

P A L E O Z O I C

* million years ago

The Mesozoic Era is often called "The Age of Dinosaurs." However, since dinosaurs were but one part of a blossoming of archosaurs, "The Age of Archosaurs" is probably a better title.

THE AGE OF ARCHOSAURS

Rhamphorhynchus
a pterosaur

Stagonolepis
an aetosaur

Many archosaur groups are extinct, so first we'll look at the Geological Time Scale. This gives us an idea of when archosaurs were around. Geologists have a number of ways of finding out how old rocks are. They have put together a Geological Time Scale with the oldest rocks at the bottom and the youngest at the top. The kinds of fossils found within the rocks of different ages allow us to divide up the Scale and give names to these divisions: Paleozoic ("ancient life") Era, Mesozoic ("middle life") Era, and Cenozoic ("recent life") Era. Many different kinds of archosaurs lived during the Mesozoic Era. The Mesozoic Era is itself divided into the Triassic Period (248 million to 213 million years ago), the Jurassic Period (213 million to 144 million years ago), and the Cretaceous Period (144 million to 65 million years ago).

The Mesozoic Era is often called "The Age of Dinosaurs." Actually, however, there were so many

Ornithosuchus
an ornithosuchid

Rutiodon
a phytosaur

Terrestrisuchus
a crocodylomorph

Plant Eating Sauropodmorphs

Meat Eating Theropods

Ornithischian Dinosaurs

Saurischian Dinosaurs

DINOSAURS

The major groups of dinosaurs. The theropods, in particular, and the ornithischians, have been important figures in the search for the origin of birds.

other kinds of archosaurs around (pterosaurs, crocodylomorphs, birds, and more) that "Age of Archosaurs" might be a better name. Archosauria means "ruling reptiles." It's a good name because archosaurs evolved into so many different kinds of animals that they truly ruled the world. There were many "experiments" during the early part of archosaur evolution, the Triassic Period. This means many different types of archosaurs appeared, but not all survived past the early part of the Jurassic Period. Crocodile-like phytosaurs, pig-snouted aetosaurs, and carnivorous ornithosuchids were all early "experiments." Crocodylomorphs, the group to which crocodiles and alligators belong, also appeared in the Triassic Period and these are still around today, of course.

Pterosaurs, the flying reptiles, first evolved in the Triassic Period and were very successful. They became extinct, however, at the end of the Cretaceous Period. Dinosaurs also first appeared during the Triassic and were successful through the rest of the Mesozoic Era. Dinosaurs can be divided into two major groups: Ornithischia, which were plant eaters, and Saurischia, which included both plant eaters and meat eaters. The meat-eating saurischian dinosaurs are called theropods and are important to the search for the origin of birds, as we'll see. At the end of the Cretaceous Period the dinosaurs, like the pterosaurs, suffered a massive extinction.

The last group of archosaurs is birds. Birds definitely appeared by the end of the Jurassic Period.

3
Archaeopteryx, Compsognathus, and the Dinosaurian Origin of Birds

About one hundred to two hundred years ago, **paleontology** was still a young science. Few fossil archosaurs had been found and most people thought birds were very different from other animals. There were some strange ideas about the origin of birds — for example, that birds evolved from turtles! Then, in 1861, workers in a rock quarry in Solnhofen, Germany, discovered an unusual fossil skeleton. The Jurassic-age sediments of the Solnhofen quarry had captured the inhabitants of an ancient lagoon. The sediments preserved anatomical details not normally found in fossils. The fossil the workers found showed clear impressions of feathers!

This was the first discovered skeleton of *Archaeopteryx*, the oldest certain bird. Six more specimens have been found since. The feathers are very similar to those of living birds, and they show *Archaeopteryx* to

An artist's view of the discovery of *Archaeopteryx*

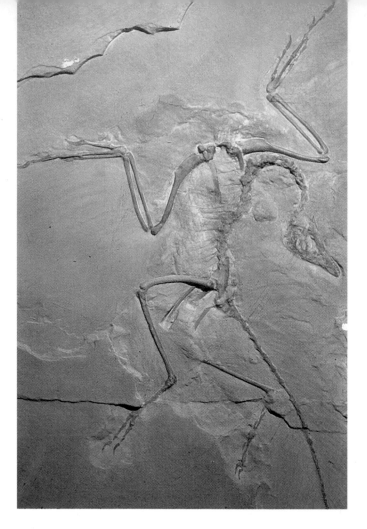

An *Archaeopteryx* fossil

be a true bird. There are other birdlike features of its skeleton, such as a wishbone, a three-fingered hand, birdlike hip bones, and a foot built for perching on tree limbs. However, *Archaeopteryx* has a larger number of primitive characters than derived bird characters; it has teeth in its jaws, a long bony tail, claws on its fingers, a simply constructed backbone, a set of bony ribs in the belly, separate hand and foot bones, and others. *Archaeopteryx* has such a mixture of primitive and derived characters that it is an almost perfect "missing link" between birds and reptiles — but which reptiles?

The Jurassic bird *Archaeopteryx* has a mixture of
primitive features and derived, birdlike features.
(See skeletal drawing on page 26.)

Dinosaurs were just beginning to be discovered in
large numbers at about the time that *Archaeopteryx*
was found. Most dinosaurs were so big that (before
Archaeopteryx) nobody had guessed these giants
might be related to birds. Then, a very small dinosaur
was discovered in the same Solnhofen rocks that
Archaeopteryx came from. This dinosaur is called
Compsognathus.

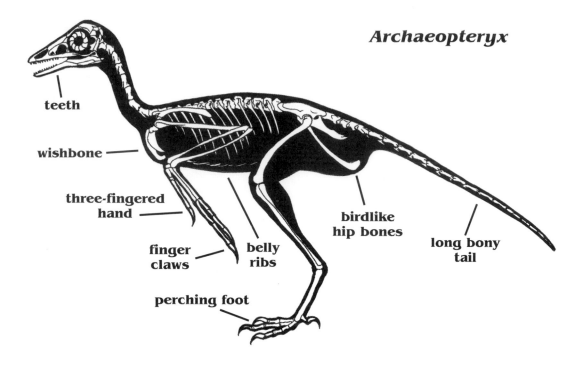

Archaeopteryx

teeth

wishbone

three-fingered hand

finger claws

belly ribs

birdlike hip bones

long bony tail

perching foot

Compsognathus was a theropod saurischian dinosaur about the size of a rooster. Paleontologists quickly saw it was a "birdlike reptile" because of its slender build, **bipedal** (two-footed) posture, and birdlike legs (especially the ankle and foot). Thus, these two Solnhofen animals, *Archaeopteryx* and *Compsognathus*, together provided a connecting link between birds and dinosaurs.

More clues for this link came from the discovery and study of another dinosaur, *Hypsilophodon*. *Hypsilophodon* had very birdlike hip bones. Although the similarities were seen in two quite different kinds of dinosaurs (*Hypsilophodon* is an ornithischian), many people began to think that birds and dinosaurs were somehow closely related. Yet not everyone agreed.

Compsognathus

The small Jurassic theropod dinosaur *Compsognathus* was the first good evidence for birdlike dinosaurs.

Hypsilophodon

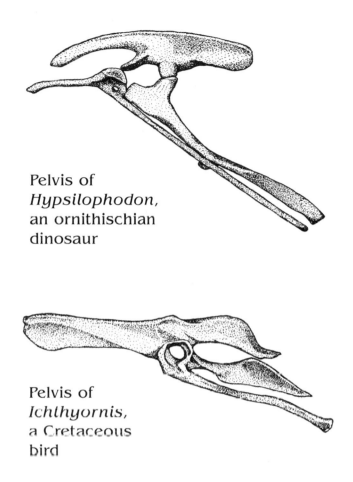

Pelvis of
Hypsilophodon,
an ornithischian
dinosaur

Pelvis of
Ichthyornis,
a Cretaceous
bird

Hypsilophodon had a pelvis similar to that of a bird.

Some paleontologists raised the issue discussed earlier: How do we know whether the similarities — in particular, being bipedal — evolved from common ancestry or from convergent adaptation to similar lifestyles? Some of these paleontologists thought that birds were related instead to pterosaurs, because both have wings.

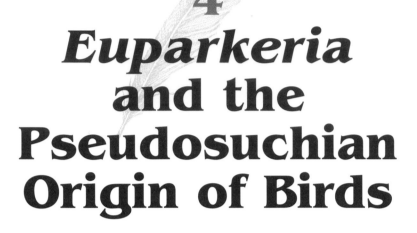

4
Euparkeria and the Pseudosuchian Origin of Birds

Although the belief that birds evolved from dinosaurs or pterosaurs became pretty popular, many paleontologists worried that these groups were too specialized to have been the ancestors of birds. For example, birds — even *Archaeopteryx* — have a wishbone. The wishbone is formed by the joining of the left and right collarbones. However, the dinosaurs and pterosaurs known at that time didn't have collarbones. So, dinosaurs and pterosaurs were thought to be too specialized to have been bird ancestors — unless birds somehow had "re-evolved" collarbones, which seemed unlikely. (Collarbones have since been found in several kinds of dinosaurs.) Many paleontologists hoped to find some different, more primitive kind of fossil archosaur, one that was not too specialized to be a bird ancestor.

In 1913, the discovery of just such an animal,

Euparkeria, a primitive archosaur from the early Triassic Period. (See skeletal drawing on page 32.)

Euparkeria, was announced. *Euparkeria* was a small carnivorous animal found in rocks of the Triassic Period in South Africa. It probably could run either bipedally or on all fours. *Euparkeria* had a collarbone, and also seemed to have no specializations that would prevent

Euparkeria

it from being ancestral to birds, and to dinosaurs and pterosaurs, too. Also, it had existed earlier than any known dinosaurs or fossil birds.

Euparkeria became the best-known member of a small group of early archosaurs called pseudosuchians. The idea that these pseudosuchians were the ancestors of birds, dinosaurs, pterosaurs, and most later archosaurs became very popular. In fact, the idea became so popular that for over fifty years the problem of the origin of birds was thought to be solved.

5
The Crocodylomorph Origin of Birds

The pseudosuchian origin of birds was not really questioned until the 1970s when a number of fresh ideas were suggested. Some of these ideas came and went quickly. One was that birds and ornithischian dinosaurs (like *Hypsilophodon*) were closely related because of similar hip bones. Most paleontologists immediately said that this similarity was surely the result of convergence and not homology.

A new theory was proposed in 1972. This suggested that the closest relatives of birds might be crocodylomorphs. It was based mostly on a primitive Triassic crocodylomorph named *Sphenosuchus*. Crocodylomorphs don't look very much like birds in outward appearance. A few paleontologists, however, saw features in the construction of the skull that resembled some features in fossil birds, such as details of the ear region, the shapes of the teeth and the way they attached to the jaw bones, and a complicated arrangement of cavities within the skull

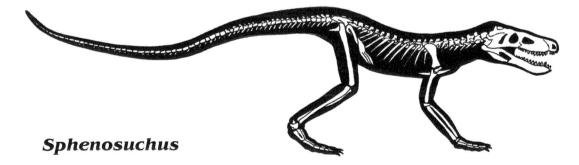

Sphenosuchus

Sphenosuchus, a primitive crocodylomorph from the late
Triassic or early Jurassic Period.

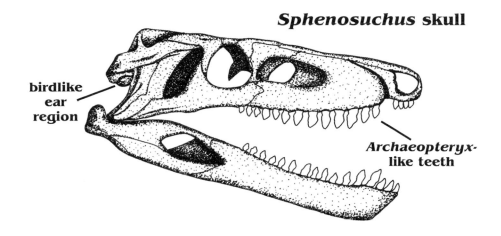

Sphenosuchus skull

birdlike
ear
region

Archaeopteryx-
like teeth

Some features of a _Sphenosuchus_, or other crocodylomorph
skull resemble features of primitive bird skulls.

bones. These similarities were certainly derived specializations. The question was, were they homologous? At the
time, few of these features had been found in other
archosaurs, such as _Euparkeria_, dinosaurs, or pterosaurs.

There are two possible explanations for these
derived similarities. First, they could be homologous.
On the one hand, this would mean that birds and crocodylomorphs are very closely related. On the other
hand, it also would mean that similarities between
birds and, say, dinosaurs (such as in the back legs)
must have evolved separately (convergence). The second explanation is that the similarities between birds
and crocodylomorphs evolved through convergence.
This would mean that birds must be closely related to
some other archosaur group.

The crocodylomorph theory has never had many
followers, probably partly because birds and crocodylomorphs are so different from each other. It's also
because a fossil was discovered that gave new life to
an old idea and generated a lot of enthusiasm.

6
Deinonychus and the New Dinosaurian Origin of Birds

Just as *Archaeopteryx, Compsognathus, Euparkeria,* and *Sphenosuchus* sparked new theories on the origin of birds, a 1969 report of the finding of a new kind of birdlike dinosaur, *Deinonychus,* triggered a fresh wave of research. *Deinonychus* was discovered in rocks from the Cretaceous Period in Montana.

Deinonychus was a small theropod saurischian dinosaur that showed some remarkable adaptations. Its powerful skull had many sharp teeth. It had strong arms with long hands armed with lethal claws. Its tail was stiff and balanced the body during its maneuvers. Its legs show that it was swift of foot. Finally, an enormous claw on the second toe of each hind foot was certainly a deadly weapon. *Deinonychus* is very closely related to *Velociraptor,* a similar theropod dinosaur from Asia.

Deinonychus

The discovery of *Deinonychus* gave new life to the theory
supporting the dinosaurian origin of birds.

Deinonychus is not all that similar to modern birds, but shows a number of close similarities to the Jurassic bird *Archaeopteryx*: the number and shapes of the openings in the snout, the positioning of the teeth in the skull, the number of fingers and the relative sizes of the finger bones, the unusual shapes of some of the wrist bones, the arrangement of the hip bones, a special kind of ankle structure, and a certain foot structure.

If we look closely at this list, we'll see that some characteristics give us more specific information about relationships than others. Some of these birdlike features (such as the ankle joint) are found in all dinosaurs, but in almost no other archosaurs. These specializations show that birds might be related to dinosaurs. Some of the features — the snout openings and foot structure — are specializations of a certain group of dinosaurs, the theropod saurischian dinosaurs. Some of the features — the positioning of the teeth, the hand and wrist structure — are found in only a few kinds of theropod dinosaurs. One feature — the hip bones — is found only in *Deinonychus* and its relatives.

These shared specializations that we see in *Archaeopteryx*, *Deinonychus*, and other dinosaurs suggest that birds indeed evolved from dinosaurs. But this idea is different from the old, original theory of dinosaur-bird relationships discussed in Chapter 3. The old version was very vague. It didn't show *which group* of dinosaurs might be closer to birds. This new theory not only says that birds evolved from dinosaurs, but also identifies a particular group of dinosaurs, the theropods. It even points to a small group of theropod dinosaurs that are most closely related to birds. There are so many derived similarities between birds and these *Deinonychus*-like theropod dinosaurs that most paleontologists today believe birds *are* theropod dinosaurs!

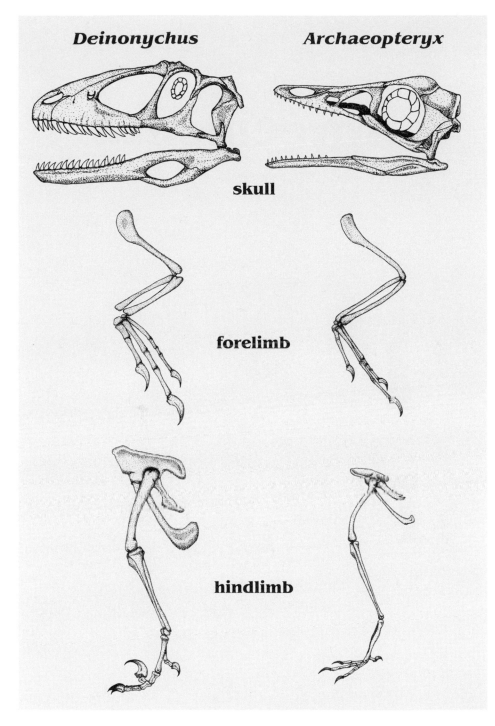

Deinonychus   **Archaeopteryx**

skull

forelimb

hindlimb

Deinonychus and *Archaeopteryx* are similar in many details of the construction of the skeleton.

7
Agreement?

The idea that birds evolved from a *Deinonychus*-like theropod ancestor is the most popular current theory. But not everyone agrees with it. The idea has been questioned for two major reasons. First, some other types of theropod dinosaurs — like *Troodon* and its relatives — might be even more closely related to birds than is *Deinonychus*.

Troodon is a small theropod dinosaur that lived during the last part of the Cretaceous Period. It's very similar to *Deinonychus*, and so this theory is not very different from the one described in Chapter 6. *Troodon*, however, has some birdlike features in its skull that aren't found in *Deinonychus* and its relatives. In fact, many of these characteristics are the ones mentioned in Chapter 5 as support for the crocodylomorph theory!

Troodon

Troodon is quite similar to *Deinonychus* and also has some
close resemblances to birds.

41

Yet *Troodon* and its relatives *lack* some of the birdlike specializations that *Deinonychus* has, such as the arrangement of the hip bones. Many paleontologists find it hard to choose between these two similar, yet quite different, ideas.

The second major objection to the new version of the dinosaurian origin of birds is the "time problem." Nearly all the birdlike theropod dinosaurs appeared *later* in time than the first bird, *Archaeopteryx*. How can an ancestor (such as *Deinonychus* or *Troodon*) be *younger* than its **descendants** (birds like *Archaeopteryx*)? It would be like your grandparents being younger than you! How can this be? There are three possible answers.

1. No one has ever thought that *Deinonychus* or *Troodon* were actual ancestors. That would be impossible. But perhaps close relatives of *Deinonychus* or *Troodon* were around in the Jurassic Period (that is, before *Archaeopteryx*) and we just haven't found them yet.

2. Maybe we've got the ancestor/descendant relationship backward. Maybe these Cretaceous birdlike theropods are actually the *descendants* of *Archaeopteryx* — that is, they're birds that have lost the power of flight!

3. It's possible that we're completely wrong about these Cretaceous theropods' being closely related to birds. Perhaps *all* their birdlike characteristics are entirely convergent.

The second possible explanation is in many ways the best. The similarities between birds and Cretaceous theropods are still homologous. The time problem is solved. However, almost no one believes this theory to

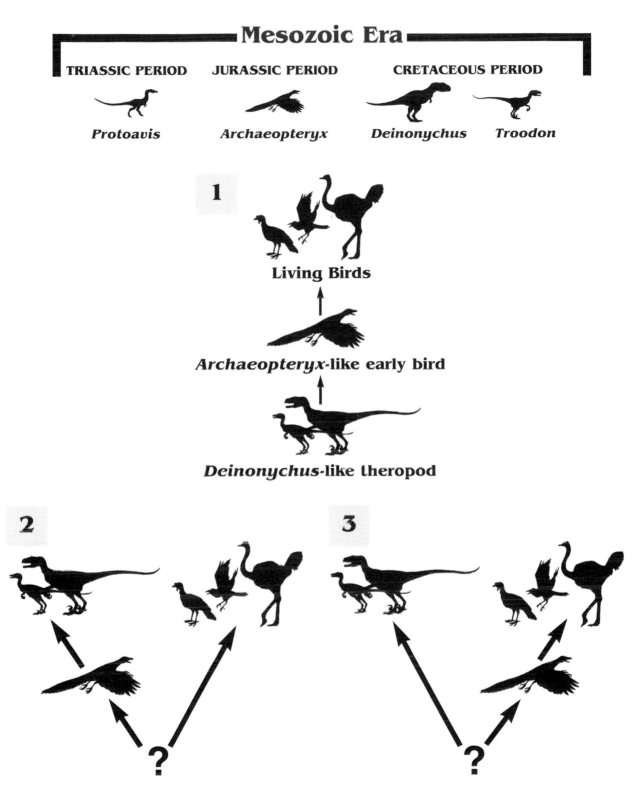

Mesozoic Era

TRIASSIC PERIOD

Protoavis

JURASSIC PERIOD

Archaeopteryx

CRETACEOUS PERIOD

Deinonychus

Troodon

1

Living Birds

Archaeopteryx-like early bird

Deinonychus-like theropod

2

3

?

?

The "Time Problem": the known birdlike theropods are *younger* than *Archaeopteryx*. **Solution 1.** *Deinonychus*-like theropods lived earlier, but have not yet been discovered. **Solution 2.** Cretaceous theropods like *Deinonychus* and *Troodon* evolved from birds like *Archaeopteryx*. **Solution 3.** The Cretaceous theropods aren't closely related to birds.

be true. *Deinonychus* and *Troodon* are so much like other theropods, in so many ways, that it is hard to believe they are actually flightless birds.

The third theory has some advantages, because some Triassic theropods like *Syntarsus* have some birdlike features. However, this would force us to believe that the many birdlike characteristics of the Cretaceous theropods evolved independently. Many paleontologists simply aren't willing to believe that so much convergence occurred.

The first theory remains the most popular. The fossil record is really not very good. Perhaps we simply haven't found the Jurassic or Triassic relatives of the Cretaceous relatives of *Deinonychus* and *Troodon*. It seems safer to accept the many similarities as homologous and hope to find some day the fossils that would provide the conclusive evidence.

The first theory, however, recently has been made harder to accept. A Triassic fossil named *Protoavis* has been discovered in Texas, and is reported to be a bird — in fact, a bird more like living birds than *Archaeopteryx*! *Protoavis* is a small, crow-sized archosaur. It does indeed show a few birdlike specializations.

Let's accept for a moment that an origin of birds from theropods like *Deinonychus* is still to be believed. We should then expect to find *Deinonychus*-like theropods in the rocks of the Triassic Period — more than 100 million years before the earliest fossils of *Deinonychus*! Because the "time problem" is so huge if *Protoavis* is really a bird, many paleontologists doubt that *Protoavis* has anything to do with birds. These *Protoavis* fossils have been discovered so recently that we're still not sure just what they mean.

In summary, the evidence comes to us in little

Living birds

Archaeopteryx

Deinonychus

Triassic or Jurassic
Deinonychus-like theropod

The most likely solution is that Cretaceous theropods like
Deinonychus share with birds a common theropod
ancestor in the Triassic or Jurassic.

pieces. Many of the clues point to different and conflicting stories. *Deinonychus* does indeed resemble the Jurassic bird *Archaeopteryx*. But what about *Troodon*? What about *Protoavis*? And what about the "time problem?" Where are the Jurassic relatives of *Deinonychus* and *Troodon*, if they existed at all? These questions still need to be answered. There are points of agreement, however. The ancestor of birds was probably a small theropod dinosaur, probably resembling *Deinonychus* in many important ways.

8
The Origin of Flight in Birds

The first thing you notice about living birds is that they can fly. The origin of flight — that is, the evolutionary steps leading to winged, feathered birds — has always been tightly linked to theories on the origins of birds themselves. This is for the simple reason that different bird ancestors provide different "starting points" down the evolutionary road to flight.

Most paleontologists who argue for the origin of birds from crocodylomorphs or other early archosaurs (such as *Euparkeria*) have thought that flight evolved "from the trees down." They believe the ancestor of birds lived in trees. To find food, these small animals leaped from branch to branch. In time, they evolved and were able to glide from tree to tree. Eventually they achieved active, flapping flight.

The Origin of Flight . . . from the trees down?

On the other side stand paleontologists who argue for the origin of birds from theropod dinosaurs, and who think that flight evolved "from the ground up." They argue that the ancestor of birds was a fast-running, ground-living animal. This ancestor used its arms for balance as it chased and leaped after insects. Eventually, these little leaps became longer and longer until powered flight evolved.

The first theory, "from the trees down," has been much more popular. It seems to make more sense. The animal doesn't need to do anything special to start on the road to flight. Gravity does all the work. Once an animal starts to fall or leap from a tree branch, anything that slows its fall — such as some long scales on its arms — will be an evolutionary advantage. Eventually, these "falls" might actually become useful leaps, allowing the animal to travel distances between trees. If the animal could control the leaps by actually gliding, the animal could travel even longer distances.

True flapping flight is the logical final step in this evolutionary sequence. While true powered flight has evolved only a few times in the history of life, many different types of animals today are good leapers or gliders. Examples include certain kinds of tree frogs,

lizards, "flying" squirrels, and "flying" lemurs. These animals, in a way, are "stuck" in the stages before true flight.

The second theory, "from the ground up," seems more difficult to believe. It would have to be true, however, if birds evolved from animals that had to stay on the ground because they were so large. Different versions of this theory have been proposed. One is that the ancestors of birds ran fast and flapped their arms to go even faster. Another version is that they ran along the ground, jumping into the air after insects. The evo-

The Origin of Flight . . . from the ground up?

lution of winglike arms helped them jump higher and farther. Still another theory suggests that the ancestors ran and jumped over logs and boulders, chasing after insects. They held their arms straight out from their sides to steady themselves as they scrambled about. All these ideas sound possible, but the theory is still hard to accept because there are so few animals living today that have such a lifestyle.

So we're faced with a problem. Fossils tell us that birds evolved directly from theropod dinosaurs. Yet common sense about the origin of flight says that it's unlikely that flight would have evolved in such animals.

What's the answer to this problem? Maybe our usual view of all theropods is wrong. Maybe the theropod ancestors of birds spent a lot of time in the trees. *Deinonychus, Velociraptor, Troodon,* and their relatives all seem to be well built for running swiftly on the ground. That doesn't mean, however, that they couldn't do some climbing, too. They certainly had strong claws and limbs. Also, as we noted earlier, none of these dinosaurs was *exactly* like their ancestor in appearance.

So perhaps the Triassic or Jurassic theropod that was ancestral to birds had many of the features that we see in *Archaeopteryx* and *Deinonychus,* but was much smaller in size and spent a lot of time in the trees, as well as on the ground. Many birds today have just such a lifestyle.

9
Conclusion: But How Do We Know?

As we noted at the beginning, the search for origins requires detective work. There are no surviving eyewitnesses to the origin of birds. The clues we get come mostly from the structure of living animals and fossils, and the fossils are usually broken and missing parts. These clues are few and often very hard to understand. In most cases, the best we can do is to come up with theories that try to explain all the clues as completely as possible. Sometimes the clues conflict and point to different theories. Then, choosing between the theories can be very difficult.

In searching for the origin of birds, we came across many conflicting clues:

Conflict: Different clues suggest different ancestors.
How do we weigh the evidence?

• The clues from the bony structures of fossils point strongly to the origin of birds from small theropod dinosaurs resembling *Deinonychus*. They don't point to crocodylomorphs or other kinds of archosaurs.

• The clues from the ages of fossils point to the origin of birds from an ancestor living in the Triassic or Jurassic periods. In other words, these Cretaceous *Deinonychus*-like dinosaurs seem to be "too late." At least crocodylomorphs and many other groups of archosaurs had evolved "in time" to be ancestral.

• Finally, the clues from theories on the origin of flight point to the origin of birds from small archosaurs that lived in trees, and not from the larger *Deinonychus*-like theropods.

How do we make sense of these clues that point us in different directions?

• The clues from the ages of fossils are not fully trustworthy. It's possible that we may someday discover *Deinonychus*-like fossils in old-enough rocks. If that happened, the "time problem" would disappear.

• The clues from the theories on the origin of flight are even less reliable. We don't know much about how these dinosaurs lived their lives. Maybe some of the *Deinonychus*-like theropods actually were small and spent a lot of time in trees.

• The most reliable clues are the ones that come from the structure of the bones themselves. They are more certain — we can look at them, measure them, hold them in our hands.

Taking all the clues together, it seems most likely that the ancestor of birds was a small *Deinonychus*-like theropod dinosaur living in the Triassic or Jurassic Period. It ran swiftly along the ground in search of food. It also spent a lot of time in the trees, maybe roosting there at night as many birds and other animals do today. Even if some of the similarities between *Deinonychus* and *Archaeopteryx* turn out to be convergent rather than homologous, it still seems certain that birds evolved from some tree-living theropod dinosaur.

So, not *all* dinosaurs became extinct at the end of the Cretaceous Period. One group of theropod dinosaurs survived. Look! One just flew by your window!

Conclusion: Birds evolved from a Triassic or Jurassic theropod dinosaur that resembled *Deinonychus* but was much smaller and, perhaps, spent a lot of time in the trees.

Glossary

anatomy: the parts of the body and their arrangement

ancestors: a group of organisms from which other groups have evolved. Ancestors must be earlier in time than their descendants.

archosaur: a group of animals that today includes birds and crocodilians, and included dinosaurs, pterosaurs, and a number of other early creatures during the Mesozoic Era

bipedal: the ability to move around on two legs

convergence: separate evolution of a similar feature in unrelated groups. The common ancestor of the groups didn't have the feature.

derived character: a feature that is "newly" evolved in a group of organisms

descendants: a group of organisms that evolved from another group. Descendants must be later in time than their ancestors.

evolution: the scientific theory that groups of organisms have changed over time and are connected to each other by lines of ancestry and descent

extinction: the total dying out of a group of organisms so that the group leaves no descendants

fossil: the remains of ancient life forms, usually found within rocks

homology: a similarity that can be attributed to common origin; a feature of different groups of organisms is homologous if the feature was found in their common ancestor

organism: a single living creature of any kind

origin: the evolutionary beginning or start of a group of organisms

paleontology: the study of ancient life. Paleontologists study fossils.

primitive character: a feature evolved usually long before the origin of a group of organisms

specialization: another word for derived character

For Further Reading

Bennett, S. Christopher, Ph.D. *Pterosaurs: The Flying Reptiles.* New York: Franklin Watts, 1995.

Benton, Michael J. *On the Trail of the Dinosaurs.* New York: Crescent Books, 1989.

Charig, A. *A New Look at the Dinosaurs.* New York: Facts On File, 1985.

Farlow, James O., Ph.D., and Molnar, Ralph E., Ph.D. *The Great Hunters: Meat-Eating Dinosaurs.* New York: Franklin Watts, 1994

Norman, David. *The Illustrated Encyclopedia of Dinosaurs.* New York: Crescent Books, 1985.

Index

Page numbers in *italics* indicate illustrations.

Aetosaurs, 21
Age of Archosaurs, the, *18*, 20
Age of Dinosaurs, the, *18*, 19
Archaeopteryx, *11*, 22–25, *23*, *24*, *25*, 26, *26*, 30, *36*, 38, *39*, *42*, *43*, 44, *45*, 46, 52, 57
Archosauria, 17–21
Archosaurs, 17, *18*, 19, 20, 21, 22, 30, 31, 32, 35, 38, 44, 47, 55
Ardeosaurus, *11*

Bats, 12–16

Cenozoic Era, *18*, 19
Common ancestry, 12, 13, 14, 29

Compsognathus, 25–26, *27*, 36
Convergence, 12, 14, 15, 33, 35, 44, 57
Convergent similarities, 14, 16, 29, *42*
Cretaceous Period, *18*, 19, 21, *29*, *36*, 40, 42, *43*, 45, 55, 57
Crocodylomorph origin of birds, 33–35
Crocodylomorphs, *19*, 20, 21, 33, *34*, 35, *35*, 40, 47, 55
Crows, 12–16
Cynognathus, *11*

Deinonychus, 36–38, *37*, *39*, 40, 42, *43*, 44, 45, 46, 52, 55, *56–57*
Derived characteristics, 14, 15, 16, 17, 24, 35, 38

Dinosaurian origin of birds, 22–29, 38

Dinosaurian origin of birds, new, 36–39, 42

Dinosaurs, *18*, 19, 21, 25, 27, 30, 55. *See also* Ornithischian dinosaurs; Saurischian dinosaurs; Theropod saurischian dinosaurs

Dolphins, 12, *13*

Euparkeria, 31–32, *31*, *32*, 35, 36, 47

Evolution, 12, 13, 17, 21, 38, 47–51

Family trees, 10, 14, 16

Feathers, 9, 16, 22, 47

Fish, 12, *13*,

Flight, 9, 12, 14, 47–52, 55, *56–57*

Flying lemurs, 50

Flying squirrels, 50

Food chain, 10

Fossils, 11, *11*, 16, 19, 22, *24*, 30, 32, 35, 44, 51, 53, 55

"From the ground up" theory of flight, 48, 50–51, *50*

"From the trees down" theory of flight, 47, 48–50, *48*, *49*, 51

Geological Time Scale, *18–19*, 19

Homologous similarities, 14, 16, 29, 35, 42, 44, 57

Homology, 12, 15, 33

Hypsilophodons, 26, *28*, 29, 33

Ichthyornis, 29

Jurassic Period, *18*, 19, 21, 22, *27*, 34, 38, *43*, *45*, 46, 52, 55, *56–57*, 57

Mammals, 9, 10, 12, *13*,

Mesozoic Era, *18*, 19, 21

Montana, 36

Ornithischian dinosaurs, *20*, 21, 26, *29*, 33

Ornithosuchids, *19*, 21

Ornithosuchus, *19*

Ostriches, 12–16

Paleontology, 22

Paleozoic Era, *18*, 19

Phytosaurs, *19*, 21

Primitive characteristics, 14, 15, 16, 17, 24

Proganochelys, *11*

Protoavis, *43*, 44, 46

Protosuchus, *11*

Pseudosuchian origin of birds, 30–32, 33

Pterosaurs, *18–19*, 20, 21, 29, 30, 32, 35

Reptiles, 17, 24

Rhamphorhynchus, 18
Rutiodons, *19*

Saurischian dinosaurs, *20*, 21, 26, 36
Sauropodmorphs, *20*, 21
Sharks, *13*
Solnhofen, Germany, 22, 25, 26
South Africa, 31
Specialization, 14, 17, 32, 35, 38, 42, 44
Sphenosuchus, 33, 34, 36
Stagonolepis, 18
Syntarsus, 44

Teeth, 9, 16, 24, 33, 36, 38

Texas, 44
Theropod saurischian dinosaurs, *20*, 21, 26, *27*, 36, 38, 40, 42, *43*, 44, 45, 46, 48, 51, 52, 55, *56–57*, 57
"Time problem," 42, *43*, 44, 46, 55
Tree frogs, 49
Triassic Period, *18*, 19, 21, 31, 33, 34, *43*, 44, 45, 52, 55, *56–57*, 57
Troodons, 40–44, *41*, *43*, 46, 52

Velociraptors, 36, 52

Wings, 12, 13, *15*, 47

About the Author

Lawrence M. Witmer, Ph.D., is assistant professor in the Department of Biological Sciences and College of Osteopathic Medicine of Ohio University in Athens, Ohio. He holds degrees from Cornell University (B.A. in biology), the University of Kansas (M.A. in systematics and ecology) and the Johns Hopkins University School of Medicine (Ph.D. in cell biology and anatomy). He is the author of many professional papers and articles and is a widely recognized authority on avian origins and anatomy.

Dr. Witmer has collected dinosaur and other fossil vertebrates in Montana, Wyoming, and Kansas, and has traveled throughout North America and Europe to study fossil specimens of birds, dinosaurs, and other archosaurs in museum collections. He lives in Ohio with his wife and young son.